AF413518

the town square

joachim matschoss

notionpress.com

INDIA · SINGAPORE · MALAYSIA

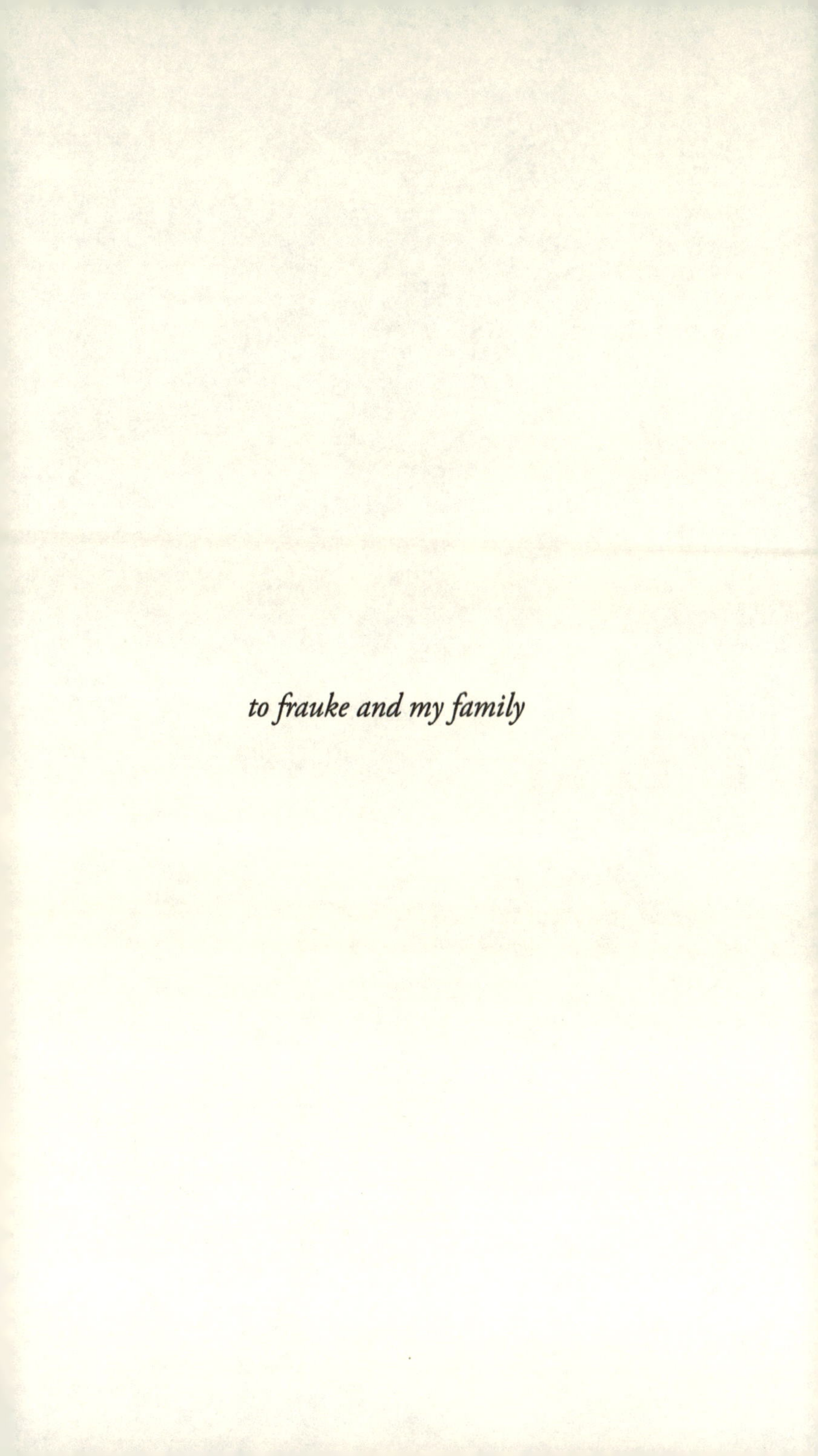

to frauke and my family

to aria

Contents

before

the lord gives and the lord takes away
so it says
but that was not right
because the lord had taken away much more
than had been there at the beginning
everything aria might have become
was now at the bottom of the hollow
waiting to be covered up
some dirt and little aria running to school
now covered up in the ground
some dirt and aria, aged ten learning the flute
now covered up in the ground
some dirt and aria tossing her hair, boys stare
now covered up in the ground
some dirt and aria, a woman traveling the world
now covered up in the ground

some dirt and aria, now ghostly old
covered up in the ground

baby aria
buried before the day was out
wrapped in cloth
so small
so very very light

below the ground

her mother walks to the cemetery
which is not far from the town square
walking alone in gentle rain
heading to that specific place
near a willow tree
grown so much taller
then she imagined it ever would be
and it is there under the bursting belly of a cloud
that she will speak to her child
aria once inside her
had wedged herself into invisibility

it is there
under that willow tree
that she cries for what would have been

knowing she was far too young
to know what to do with aria

she calls out
how to keep a life alive

she calls out
what is on the other side

she calls out
there is nobody in the cemetery
nobody apart from the rain
the rain and the willow

after

what could have been the cause
the blanket: too thick
was she sleeping on her back
maybe aria choked
was sick and nobody knew
the door to her room was shut
who would have heard her cry
her mother was too young
to know what to do

what else did happen

her mother took the blanket out of the cradle
pulled off the pillowcase
put away the mobile with the stars
and pushed the cradle into a corner

now she sits down
forever wondering why

as life goes on around her

paths

you will get there
just be patient
wade through a river
because you will not find a bridge
but you will get there
walk across the mountain pass
because you will not find a tunnel

and suddenly there it will be
the old gate
transparent in the sunlight
you'll see windows and balcony doors
shadows of people seeming to dance
or maybe swimming beneath chandeliers
look a little further
don't be afraid

rusting sheet metal
planks with spikes
piles of tins
fading signs of better times
frames of staved-in straw chairs
withered ropes
not even good enough to hang yourself
aria lives nearby
sometimes she climbs high up her willow
looking across to the mountains

gossip

come, make an effort

look across the square

imagine its past glory

the sun is on your back

as it always has been

take notice of the sound of horses on the cobbles

and welcome the whispers of sweet nothings in the streets

even though the scents of sewage hitchhike the breezes

that swirl around the houses and its people

eavesdrop to expired gossip as it seeps into memory

everyone here must have been young once

like spring

it surely would have been infectious

even magical

to be alive against the odds

and not detained by the roots of a willow

circles

in the middle of the square

you are its heart

everything grows around you in concentric circles

like tree trunks adding one ring each year

but in the land of the perished

the cemetery

there you will age differently

on fine afternoons the dead

take out their magnifying glasses

to decipher their names on stone slabs

their own names

aria knows her name

she knows that the unborn just whisper

she knows about necks that are thrust out

she knows about mouths that will always stay shut

so that they will avoid suffocation from the dust

and she knows that the roots of a willow

will keep her safe for another life

daisy

the sun throws a glance
across the crammed cemetery
in case you're wondering
you'll find it behind the church since time began –

the dead must really feel at home
now that the soil has warmed up, even deep below
a mist of loss seeps from the borrows of the worms
settles on the blades and roots of grass
and those who came here to mourn
marvel at the pretty dress that this very day is wearing
and there under a willow tree
two little fingers hold a daisy

rain

look, over there, under the railway bridge
still dripping with last night's rain
dozens of low-life doves adorn the girders
and those beneath
those beneath they walk faster
afraid of shit in hair and
streaks of slime on sleeves
the town's complained
the whole country did
even aria whispered from below the willow
pleading to the authorities
but nothing has been done
ever

tiny feet

her mother stirs in morning's quiet
she can hear tiny feet patter
now the world has awoken
aria can hear coffee dripping
her mother hears a clock ticking
and like always, she'll be bracing against the day —

within years lunches will be packed
a myriad of kisses given
love
unspoken
vast
endless

and now

when evenings come

stories will be shared

and sleepy eyes eventually close

all in a mother's gaze

past curtains

past a cobbled street

and past the town square

lightyears past the dreams of tomorrow

patterns

sometimes aria's gaze runs over patterns
that follow one another like in a musical score
not a single note can be changed because
the secrets of the square lie in these patterns

listen

walk along the streets that branch off
in all directions like a starfish
there, can you hear the copper clock
that follows the barber's striped awning
can you see the fountain with its seven jets
five of them blocked up since time began
the melon vendor's cart rattles on the cobbles
the statue with the meercat and the mouse
covered by a day of pigeon's bowels work
the bakery closed
the church empty
the cemetery full

and the willow tree silent

ah, the silence

in-between

another day of wallowing
of waking up in tears
picking at little flakes of skin
just around her nails
avoiding bleeding
avoiding well
telling herself that as long as you're breathing
there is more alive than
there is more right than wrong

aria's mother walks to work
follows the traces of her fears
another day of in-between
the worries and the unfair
caught amidst the hopeless and the mean
all she wants is a life for aria

she had milk for weeks
milk for the baby in the ground

colin

look over there

see how aria points at a sleepwalker

the one in the purple pyjamas

see how he slowly circles the fountain at the centre of the
square

his feet seem shrouded in soot and grease

he must've come from colin

the motor mechanic from manchester

colin's cars just around the corner

he took aria's mother to a wine bar

but only for one evening

because her mother liked the wine much more than colin

the wine bar is right next to carla's cheeserie

whose smell fights the odour

of the saddler's shop two doors down

leather, camembert and merlot

let's look at every house

the secrets

stories told in whispers

come walk

follow aria

and believe

falsehood is never in words

it is in things

the spire

look to the left
yes, towards the church
for most of the day
the spire of that church
casts a sword-like shadow across the square
seemingly harpooning those in its way
lucia the black cat detests shadows
she seems to salivate for pure sun
sitting on the wall with its ancient bricks
waiting for cat loving tourists
dropping croissants crumbs
aria likes lucia
because on some days
she would follow her
all the way to school

the doll

aria would have been five or so

and every time she enters the square

she will find herself in a dialogue

with either herself

or her old rag doll

melania

a foolish servant she takes to places

but only on days without rain mshe is over one hundred years old

handed down from daughter to niece

and further to son and to nephew

melania played all the parts she was ever cast in

in an epic play called 'childhood'

snow

snow begins to settle
on the black boughs of the great chestnut
aria wants to be a child
made of snow under a sky
weary
tired of light

soon snow falls gently like a silky curtain
everything becomes slow and quiet

aria can see life more clearly
like through a magnifying glass:

the dark days

the blows around her mother's eyes

the blankets made from snow

the pillows made from ice

spring

earth will crack open

and spring

well spring

will properly spring

and in the barren landscape

crocuses push into light

and the town will open its mouth

but, aria, please don't cry

dance until your bones will laugh and clatter

you are alive

sing

sing

and you will rise

summer

in high summer the streets are full of fire
aria likes the sun
she likes how it tickles her skin
how it rips right through the clouds
rays cascading from another universe
aria likes the sun
because on those days she can sip cold lemonade
that her mother will buy from the little store
over there, just near the townhall
it's an old family recipe
passed down through the generations
that have owned the store
ever since carriages pulled by horses
graced the cobbles —

the juice of one lemon

a leaf of mint

a handful of snow

a smile

and if you like a small dream

winter

just above
aria's mother opens the window
to let the sea breezes in
that fill her lungs with salty zest
she wails like a town crier
from a cloud-capped tower
her screams can be heard most mornings
with time she'll grow tired
sit on a chair and reach across to a basket
and will continue knitting a pair of little gloves
for years she hopes to give them to the child
but one winter fades into the next
if she would look up
she could see tiny fingers
reaching up through frozen soil
under a willow tree

dream

just last night
aria dreamt of being lost on barren land
a vast landscape dotted with meteorites
erratic boulders
in the distance the spires of a town
slender pinnacles made in such a way
the moon in her journey
could take a little rest on one of them
and maybe later even on another
looking like a giant lollypop

she believes that
you can grow in lightness
if you tiptoe across the clouds

miranda

and there goes miranda
she was in aria's class in year 10
left school soon after
there around the corner
there she is
can you see her
worn-out heels
pink-rimmed specs
she's early today
heading to her spot under the crumbling balcony
waiting for those that head to the alley at dawn
along there the streetlights are all broken
darkness hides the secrets
and miranda's near nakedness
she has a little chequered bag
her life is all in there

ramen

for a while the little street
that branches off from the square to the southeast
that street was called dumpling alley
a woman from hongkong
she cooked for aria
when her mother couldn't

because she was held back at work
held back by life

ramen noodles, churros and dumplings
made from what was left
a pinch of saffron
a dash of sumac
teaspoon of ajwarin or mahlebi

the woman from hongkong smiles
and as always
there is the echo of love

even bites

on certain days people
in the lanes and alleyways
that branch off from the square
are all behaving like strangers
it's the moon's fault
aria imagines a myriad of things
meetings take place
conversations
smiles
caresses
even bites
not a word is spoken
no one says hello
eyes might lock for a moment
then dart away, moving, always

away from the truth of being lonely

aria's mother doesn't go outside

not on those days

she watches a spider

catching a fly

dirt

two girls return from school
aria knows them
but they don't know her
don't know the willow
don't know dirt is in every cavity
her mouth
her ears
even the sockets of her eyes
the girls are twirling taylor swift umbrellas
cheekily on their shoulders
even though there is not a sign of rain
and over there two other girls
twins dressed in green and orange
something runs between them
invisible lines connect them
arrows

stars

triangles

until all combinations are used up

aria crosses the road

in that moment after school

walks home

alone

a little bit of dirt

falls off her shoulders

lucia

unannounced

lucia returns from her morning prowl

everyone apart from aria believes

she is the most horrible cat

in the neighbourhood

lucia is a scratcher of dogs

a slayer of all living things

look there she is

fat and sleepy

on the steps to the patisserie

aria looks across and dreams

that one day

if the stars align

she might be able to taste

a warm waffle with ice-cream

tall man

down near the river on a grassy bank

a very tall man stands very still

he is covered in tattoos

staring at round shaped glowing things high above

aria believes he looks at stars because

he must have fallen from the milky way

the tall man wears fluorescent gumboots

and proclaims he knows copernicus —

oh, a boy on a unicycle dashes through his legs

he drops something

and a young man with white hair picks it up

aria knows it was a ball and not a star

now a blind man with a dalmatian on a leash

moves slowly around the fountain

where the cobbles are treacherous

a little further on a woman with an ostrich-plume fan
smiles

aria has heard her read poems on a sunday

in the french café not far from here

aria likes the poems

especially the one about the day

when the circus came to town

and a tall man had fallen from the sky

pietro

once a year aria leaves the willow
and goes to the delicatessen
although pietro's shop is mainly for the tourists
selling local cheeses and the famous sausage
pietro says the fountain should have been named after
this item of cylindrical length full of minced pork
and it would have been if it weren't for neptune —

once a year aria is allowed a cheese sandwich
melty, stingy, gooey, even a little chewy
with tomato, sliced onion, spices, peppers
once a year on the day
when aria's father did finally leave the house
and never returned

claws

lucia squirms, rolling on her back
just as a stranger looks at her
soon he will be very close
aria smiles, knowing what will happen
lucia's coy and sweet
maybe even hungry for a little love
the stranger reaches for her belly
she flicks the tip of her tail
and like a snake striking
she sinks fifteen teeth
and a hundred claws into flaky white skin
leaving a mark right next to a tattoo stating:
invincible

lucia growls

the stranger howls

and aria

aria just smiles

the young

the young are out

it's sunday

there they are

neatly folded on the tired steps to the church

reminiscing the seductions from the night before

the cheap red wine

and dreams of copulation

the innocent orgy

without a word exchanged

now fingers fly over phones

breathlessly foraging for emojis

nobody looks up

struggling with what face to choose

or maybe just a plain red heart

that's more like love

aria looks on from a distance
from deep below
she doesn't have a phone
the willow whispers, look
and through the soil
she can see beautiful red poppies

the baker

a couple of boys
school uniform in tatters
fading like their future
aria saw them steal a bag of gavottes
they seem to find refuge behind bins
oh no
the baker chases them
wielding a baguette
snapping it on the head of the smallest boy
who screeches in f sharp
his voice not broken yet
but the baguette has, in half
sparrows twitter on the roofs
jump, flutter, maybe even fly
always on the hunt for crumbs

mirror

two doors down from the bakery
a couple of steps will lead
to a one-room-hardware-store
a hoarse bell rings when you open the door
step inside and look into the large mirror
aria went there often when she was little
staring at her reflection
hoping to catch a glimpse of the past
but all she could see was a willow
and dirt raining down in spades

the mirror reflects everything that is on sale

sometimes increasing its value

other times denying it

it all depends on the light

not everything seems valuable when mirrored

probably because it isn't

come in but be careful

put one foot in front of the other

and don't knock anything over

centuries

they look tired
the houses all around the square
worn-out by history
centuries of decadence
plagues that emptied them out more than once
collapsing beams reducing them to rubble
occasionally survivors emerged from the basements
swarming little rats to rummage and gnaw
months of poverty followed
but eventually life returned
with its heartbeat and its breath

aria marvels at the little balconies that survived

the archways and the life going on behind windows

she loves the juggler with the red nose

and the blind woman singing verdi

coffee

coffee is always a hit

in the little corner shop

one eye on the square

the other on the cup or the mug

the morning kisses you

coffee pierces the throat

and eyes shoot to euphoria

tongues warm

minds cool

now the mug dips a little

pouring pure comfort

it listens

it breathes

even loves

blue

look southwest

look seaward

can you see the balcony with the red umbrella

climb up the trellis on the left

then over the railing, it's not high

the door is open, always

up there you will find a crystal globe in every room

gaze into each of them

come on, don't be shy

can you see the blue city

have a look from all angles

dive into the blue, headfirst

and everything will match your desires

your dreams

your everything

and whatever you imagine will be possible

be quick

because in a moment

it will be possible no longer

sapporo

just for a couple of years
some time ago
a young couple from sapporo
took over a former greengrocer's
and opened a ramen place
they worked day and night
taking care of everyone who was hungry

broth, eggs, a handful of spinach
on special days cabbage slices
nori flakes, shiny green peas
gave it dignity
a bridge to japan —

their handful of customers
knew that ramen isn't a stage one grows out of —

but one november morning
early snow had fallen
aria noticed a sign
under new management
and soon the smell of organic pizzas took over

laura

early in the morning
you can find laura in the alleyway
that branches off just behind the chemist
it's a dead end
laura is tall, quite slim
wearing her everyday disguise
navel-and-nose-and-ear-and-lip-pierced
red doc martens and khaki
lovely like a new rose, if only
laura waits for her dealer
who has her money in his pocket
and she his promise in her veins

they were in the same class once
at lunchtime laura shared her sweets
and aria her carrots and the celery

breezes

aria glances at the clouds
high above the square
she spots a big mac wrapper
and there, two blue plastic bags
slowly waltz together
how they twirl and dip
and soar and lift
fills her with wonder
and she knew that one day
she will be able to dance on sea breezes
with a salty smile

chickens

grade four could have been one of the best years
the primary school had two chickens
and aria was made the monitor of roxy and foxy
she was in charge of everything
even if just for a little while
one night the moon hung low
a few stars watched the events unfold below:
a jackal was on the hunt
sneaking around with lowered back and risen ears
burrowing into the coop
pushing fox-snout and fox-body through the hole
and in a frenzy killing them both

the teacher spoke at the burial

calling them heroes, the hens

and that the whole thing wasn't aria's fault

and foxy was the wrong name for a chicken anyway

all the children nodded

wondering if roxy was a better name

a week later two hamsters arrived

aria didn't like them

and from that day on

she didn't pay a visit to the school

even though the willow always whispered that she should

luigi

luigi's family owned the second-hand shop for centuries

even before the earthquake

even before the plague

the famine, the great fire and the flood

and what you can find here

is as old as time

silverplated forks and oh those spoons

a chess set with the black queen gone

and there, near the step a couple of unhappy houseplants

shoes that must have belonged to dead men

a one-handed breast pump

wooden nothings

and a manual that explains eternity

look, there in the corner
a faded photograph
of a willow in light rain

kia

around the corner comes a kia soul

can you hear

it's a car but I'm sure you knew that

its tyres raise a fine grey dust off the cobbles

and be assured that in no time

that dust will sneak in through the windows

curl up in and beyond the key holes

rise through the floorboards

and settle on tables to season the food

it will dry out your eyes

and it will line your lungs

now the soul is gone

the car that is

the dust remains

and over there aria picks up a damp cloth

to wipe the table

old box

aria will find letters
she'll find faded photographs
inside an old box
that is under her mother's bed
and in one of the letters
her grandfather
a kind man she had never met
wrote that a cigar under the night sky
is like a friend who listens and knows
that when the smoke has vanished
the essence will still remain just as life does
aria doesn't like cigars
or smoke, not even the box
but she would have loved life,
its essence and its fragrances

the book

a duke stood on his balcony
behind the ornamental balustrade
centuries ago
it was a feature of his palace —

he watched with concentration
how his empire grew
proud that the line of boundaries had expanded
embracing conquered territories
he marvelled at the farms he took over
all the little towns
all those villages

he saw caravans of slaves shift mountains of marble
to make his palace shine
a place crammed with wealth
crammed with ornaments and offices
he made life difficult with structure and senseless
hierarchies —

and one day the people said no longer

aria did read about all this in a history book
she liked the bit about the empire being crushed
crushed by its own weight

see how she smiles
and there, look
how she closes the book

hotel

the only hotel right on the square
is oh so very proud that its guests
wake every morning between fresh sheets
and wash with just-unwrapped cakes of soap
dry with stark-white towels
and reach into a fridge
the latest model
to take out still unopened minibar surprises
see how they smile
and dance into the lift
where synthesizer warble
and lavender fumes cradle

down below, in aria's world

lucia growls

and life is very different

there, half-squeezed tubes of toothpaste

old newspapers on which an ass was wiped

plastic wrappings

food scraps

shattered glass

broken dreams

all things discarded

strangle life running out of breath

on trend

clickety, clickety
the sound of dice falling
two old men play backgammon
aria is certain she would beat them both
if it weren't for the willow
the willow and the dirt
two hipsters watch in silence
they live in the house with the red letterbox
make pasta with pesto early evenings
and drift like ghosts after dawn
through art deco bars
to feast on wine and tapas

next month one of them will take up a new job
four hours away by train
very soon they will have different partners
maybe anna or antonio
there will be new pastimes
don't call it a hobby
they will make new friends who love the talking heads
but it is so very hard to stay on trend
yet for a while they both will try hard
to look like david byrne

emma

aria sits on the steps of the fountain
she holds a twig from a willow tree
and watches a gaggle of blackbirds
that frequent the fringes of a pergola
as pigeons work the cobbles
in search for a quick brunch

nearby, a parking meter officer
is fixed on finding culprits
she lifts window wipers with glee
and sticks messages on windscreens

emma arrives with a bunch of purple tulips

which she did buy for her mum

she notices the message

cradled by a tired wiper-arm

curls her lips and shakes her head

a curse towards the officer

a snarl towards the pigeons

another day to forget

franco

he sings badly

loafing on an old camping stool

and his guitar misses a string

still aria gives him an ear of patience

because franco sang the ave maria

when they slipped her beneath the willow

she drops some coins into his strawhat

the very few she's got in her pocket

left over change from the day

when she paid the ferryman

who helped her crossing over

franco loved singing for aria and her mother

who never paid any attention to him or his songs

he dreams of an island

where days have no agenda

you can dance barefoot

and nobody cares if f-sharp

is the seventh semitone of the solfege or not

the dog

the little skinny black dog
leaves its mark at the lamppost
but pop-eyed from constipation
it has a hump from trying to, you know
now it circles the fountain
zigzagging boots stampeding on the cobbles
two weeks later it was found dead
only aria cared to bury it
carrying it down to the river
putting it to rest near a willow
leaves cling and grow pale in an instant
and its weeping limbs are heavy with sorrow

bakery

stars still tease the clouds

and the moon is still in charge

although lights in the bakery are already on

tickling pockets of darkness

there walks a man alone

with a suitcase in his hand

unsure of where to go

maybe the first cup of coffee

will tickle his senses into an upright now

and he will urge the night to rest

soft and silent

and in freshly washed pyjamas

listen

now there are voices coming from the bakery
words like yeast and dough and flour
and in the silence underneath the willow
aria hopes a croissant might find its way

violin

he holds her like a newborn
this instrument of hollowed wooden frame
laced with five strings made of gut
now he draws the bow of hair
crosswise over strings tuned in perfect fifths
he has made violins for years
ever since his father stopped making them
because of arthritis and bad eyes
he calls it an instrument of peace
and sometimes he still plays and plays and plays
and there is aria
sitting on her schoolbag
listening to faint whisperings
of a willow
near a river

river

along the river willows dip
and trail their branches in the water
in late autumn they'll begin to quiver
dance on the ripples and ravines like ghosts
afraid of winter's harsh grip
around here lucia hunts for mice
and in early spring miranda
with chequered bag
dangles her feet in the current
dreaming of a life
free from men

tok tok tok

some say the spirit of this place
lives in the depths below the square
in blue-black underground lakes
others say it lives at the edge of wells
or in the slender arches of the aqueducts
maybe even in the blades of windmills
or hides in the canes of the blind
that tap across the cobbles
tok tok tok
aria is certain that it breathes underneath a willow
this spirit
gently swaying in the breeze

luiz

a little further on
there is a wall and a rickety bench
old men sit there to reminisce
trying to remember the time before the war
watching the young go by
in floral granny dresses and fringed vests
they too think of other times
when they hadn't even been born yet
and bellbottoms and cutoffs were the rage

a little further on in a quiet cul-de-sac

there is a little restaurant

luiz cooks pheasant there

over a fire of seasoned cherry wood

it smells delicious, would taste even better

see how he sprinkles marjoram over golden flesh

now he waits for someone to try it

but the young walk straight past

holding protein shakes in one hand

and a phone in the other

streets

when you look down into the streets

through faint stained-glass roses

there below these windows

the pavement is varied and foot-worn

cobbles, slabs, gravel and blue-white tiles

eclectically mixed and everywhere

surprises to your view

and now, can you hear it

behind the square the river whispers

of bridges, each different from the next

covered some

on pillars others

suspended even

sometimes, gargoyle-like faces seem smitten

when aria walks past

she will make sure

that no ghost can catch her

wine

lucia's father declares himself sober
shortly after he opens a little wine bar
right next to the sushi place
he does daily tastings
in secret
not the sushi
just the wine
lucia's mother can still feel the vicious blows
thrown engulfed in boozy haze —

the wine bar is long closed now
the scars remain
he has vanished so they say
but aria has seen his ghostly self
balancing along the wall of the cemetery
shouting words like sorry
but the wind turned
and took him and sorry away
far away

francesca

around the square you can find rarely gardens

not even patches of soil

just the odd, lonely flowerpot

but around a corner is a shop

full of colour and scent

and the beauty of spring

you can't miss it

cascades of glowing posies

violets and daffodils and roses

the joy of bloom gives glow and warmth

to streets born from grey cobbles

francesca works there

opens and closes the shutters every day

looks after aria when her mother can't

on other days

she carries a tin bucket with white lilies

all the way to the willow

or make wreaths for tragedies that are yet to come

sweep up fallen stems and petals

later she'll pull the door with a little force

so that it safely shuts

and watch the sun fold for another day

piano

hidden behind an old cherry tree
aria can sometimes feel vibrations
wobbling
warping
getting hauled back to pitch and harmony
the piano tuner
he comes here often
to cradle the ancient instrument
miguel is a melody mechanic
an interpreter of intervals
an ageing bird making a nest for songs
that nobody has ever heard
but hands will ask to play them later
caressing the shiny keys of the piano
and soon a fountain sings
and cobbles dance

luigi

he sits on a green plastic chair
outside the laundromat
watching his clothes somersault in the dryer
pieces of giggling fabric
dizzy from all the spin and tumble
and there, to your left, a man eats cake
while cycling across the cobbles
a woman folds t-shirts
her eyes glued to the nipples
of a young man in silk shorts
jogging slowly on the footpath
he listens to music and sings softly
aria wonders if her clothes will ever be clean
from all the dirt and the remnants of the willow —

an hour later luigi folds his underwear
odd-shaped, like dreams
the silky young man and the folding woman
are nowhere to be seen

and aria listens to her jumper
laughing quietly into its sleeves

fish

the fishmonger, hands like flounders,
loads a basket of sea urchins on a cart
fifty years ago he was already old
or maybe those that know him are mistaken
no longer amongst the living
his resemblance dissolving in advancing tides
he is just an alien face
beaming anguish
but behind him if it is him
a woman weighs lobsters
she too resembles someone
who has been spotted at midnight
dancing around a willow
with damp feet from dew
or the ripples of a nearby lake

we all reach a moment in life when

among the people we have known

the dead outnumber the living

frog

last autumn a frog mistook the fountain for a pond
and coins thrown by tourists for good luck
mistook them for crumbling parts of insects
even the delicacy of crunched up flies
over the next few weeks
children heard good night stories
about a blonde-locked prince
who had been transformed by magic
into a frog swimming in senseless circles
at the base of a fountain
always under neptune's gaze

aria does not believe those tales
under the light of the last stars
you can see her diving for coins

natalie

she sweeps the cobbles
outside the door of the patisserie
the same old crumbs like every other day
flaky skin from tired croissants
the stale bits from proud baguettes
even creamy blobs from pompous pastry offerings
natalie carries another year on her shoulders
she is as old as her broom
who has seen the dust of time
seven decades heavy

frida

stepping into frida's hair salon
feels like a romantic comedy
which editors have forgotten to groom
frida's from oslo
once dreamt of winning eurovision
frida has been cutting hair for decades
her scissors attract the true believers
the true believers in love
and those tired of life
on some days the infirm with their mobile dating help
and the sad ones
there are the angry birds
but the one unifying characteristic is always loneliness —

frida will cut them all to size
blow-waves them back to reality —

aria has never come to see frida
she has the worms
to keep her hair in shape

nails

fantasia's nails is wedged in the laneway
behind the noisy seven-eleven and the atm
she is known for her acrylics
baby-pink french tips that sparkle
but carol
she wants coral
even though it will look wrong
because it will clash with carol's new engagement ring
her daughter, skinned knees and bug bites
asks for yellow polish on her toenails
carol tells her she should get baby-pink
I'm no barbie, the daughter wails
knowing yellow and hope
are almost the same thing

scents

what wafts across from of the organic fruit shop
competes with the odour of overflowing bins and dog turds
but step through the door
and heavenly bells will ring
the trickle of jasmine will cradle your nose
mangoes are soft and yellow here
and strawberries silent like sweet kisses
peaches glow like the breasts of venus
and plums shine like a maiden's elbow
side by side in snug closeness
here, everyone dreams of fruit salad
blobs of cream
and time walking very slowly

vanessa

she is from sicily
married a man from cologne
two years later he divorced her
karl-heinz blamed money-issues
he was one of a dozen real estate agents
in his buried habitat around the fountain
and its maze of lanes and streets
rent – sell – lease
vanessa loves clothes and jewellery and shoes
the van of the amazon man parks permanently
around the corner from the apartment
karl-heinz dies six months after the divorce
then vanessa dies

the van is gone

someone else owns the flat

the real estate office is shut

live-rent-sell-lease-decease

jenny

her shoes are worn and weathered
she circles the fountain day-in, day-out
trying to resist the pull of the red door
penelope's shop is called 'addiction'
bright purple fairy lights around the ruby entry
floors, shiny like polished grapes
tempting those in need of love
what you see in penelope's world
has never been owned before
the tease of something new
jenny will buy
will buy
will buy
just to fill the blue

luciano

deodorant and sweat waltz slowly in luciano's gym
francesca is here almost every day
does her sit-ups in her skin-coloured leggings
to flatten the stomach and make the belly-button ring
skip
loves her thighs but not her calves
her weight adjustment is set low
she knows who will look at her
smiling on the rowing machine
adjusting hair and bra straps
later she'll perspire a little on the treadmill
but on the leg press she'll just tie her shoelaces
which are fluorescent and pink

francesca often watches sparrows
fighting for crumbs on the cobbles
dreams of dancing
held really close
she looks at her phone
swipes left
swipes right
swipes right
swipes left

she smiles at luciano
knowing it will never lead to anything

soon she'll return home
switch on netflix
and eat something from the freezer

milan

see, over there
that's milan's store
step on the carpet
laid out in symmetrical motives
patterns repeated along straight lines
interwoven with intoxicatingly coloured spikes
repeated and repeated and repeated
look carefully and you will see worn-out steps
winding lanes
dead ends
balconies
little windows
and faintly you can hear the trickle of a fountain
wearing a cobbled necklace around its watery head
and somewhere over there is aria
diving for coins

young

he sits on the step of the fountain, pen in hand
the coffee is getting cold
a girl walks by, twirling an umbrella on her shoulder
but it isn't raining
nor does the sun shine brightly
a woman in a black dress shows her full age
under a veil she looks at her with restless eyes
her lips tremble
she whispers something about philosophers
that only give value to youth
later the woman will go to the library
crawl inside a cover of a bronte novel
pull the pages up to her neck
and dream of parasols and adolescence

nelson

obscured by a cloud of smoke
nelson lays on the floor in the tobacco shop, dazed-eyed
his lips glued to an opium pipe
occasionally he makes the sound of horses
imitate the cracking of whips
later luisa will ride past, thighs naked
she will reach the cemetery soon

aria saw nelson often hide in a tomb
playing his flute like pan
hoping that other graves might answer

soup

the place aria calls home has no name
neither has the soup she likes the most
navy beans
sliced potatoes
onions with lots of salt and pepper
honey
horseradish
corn
oh corn
she eats that soup under the family tree
a willow
and dreams of her mother

garden

there is a little garden
on either side of the school's gate
there are flowers
their scents have been lost over time
dogs relieve themselves here
before and after school
before and after dinner
occasionally someone puts seedlings into the ground
hoping for the tree of life to grow
but time has long been barren
a bell rings
and a horde of children
tramples over anything that still remotely is alive
two girls, pony-tailed, marvel at what tik tok has to say

aria holds a little blue watering can
in the hope to rescue what barely is still breathing

mirandolina

the minute mirandolina steps into the shoe store
which is around the corner from the library
everyone knows she will not make up her mind
about what will make her feet feel most at home
shoes stare wide-eyed a her
smile toe-teasingly
looking desirable to be worn
flicking their eyelashes —

the glossy and the oh so sexy sandals
but footwear is so hypocritical
trying to please while torturing mind and feet —

angelo, the boyfriend demands heels
just so she will seem taller
but she can't walk in them
the ground seems to always shake
in truth, she feels smaller, always
praying for recognition
and a beauty that a magazine tells lies about —

aria is glad not to have the problems
of those that are still living

roberto

roberto walks backwards in the evenings
just to remember what happened that day
backwards on the painful cobbles
his worn-out shoes collecting bagfuls of stones
the alleyways and streets and squares
they don't remember him
tripping
stumbling
all over the pavement
blister red

home

listen, yes you
so you can hear what aria has to say
about this town
the square
the streets and the alleyways
the proverbial virtues
the faults and eccentricities
the obsessions
the disregard for rules
life planted at random
colourless
without character
and yet at certain hours
under certain light
in certain places along the streets

or on certain cobbles somewhere on the square

suddenly it is right in front of you

something unmistakable

rare

this feeling of home

morris

morris is now finally really really cool
he left home
he left school
he sleeps long
he sleeps very long
he gets up late
skips online lectures
plays minecraft with his mates
morris drinks tequila
morris drinks beer
and occasionally gin
and he and pornhub are in sinc and sin
morris hasn't worked at all since june
and aria knows that nothing will happen anytime soon

agnes

oh, there she is, over there
under the chestnut-tree
agnes does not want to spend one more minute
waiting for maurizio to call her back
she doesn't know that he had lost his phone
while doing a handstand at a yoga retreat
of course, payphones are so last century
maurizio does not know how to write a letter
he is an emoji kinda guy
and even if he could put pen to paper
the post office is only open fridays
and today is saturday —
sweet agnes, she is really bored
she'll soon head to a bowling alley
or the virtual escape room
to strike up new friendships

options

sergeant battoni strongly believes
and strong he is
that ninety percent of a policeman's workload
deals with things that didn't happen
but last night someone apparently heard screaming
the sound of real anguish
a person in extreme distress
but maybe it was just
coming from a bar down the hill
bad karaoke
sergeant battoni puts the kettle on
and ponders all his options
he'll wait for his colleague to return
who he did send to the bakery
to get some tit bits that would go well with tea

biscuits, maybe even cream cake
he will keep the windows closed
won't be able to hear the screams
and the blows and the wailing

freddy

little freddy loves the fountain
especially in summer
he likes to splash and dive for coins
if only he knew that aria has them all
freddy fills balloons with water and throws them at girls
he used to love dragons, even fairies
but now he likes to put snorkels on his army men
steal ken and barbie from his sister
or put play-doh into the ears of his cat
lucia will soon make him bleed
from sharp-clawed scratches
she will growl
and he will sulk
pick up his g.i. joe

and throw it in the fountain

aria will pick it up that night

and place it carefully near the willow

and cover it with dirt

moths

a few metres down from the library

there is a place as old as time

grief-skinned widows meet here once a week

for some kind of comfort

a knitted shawl

a nap

even faith

time rarely moves here

two small moths can vouch for that

there they are

just above the window

grey flecks on pale paint

there are holes in widows' cardigans

but the moths never feasted there

time did

they sit idle in a nest of balls of wool
knitting
one loop after another
hoping to stitch together the holes
buried deep inside of them

music

next to the wool-shop is the record store
bells sing as you open the door
there's the smell of dusty vinyls
lounging in age-old shelves
be gentle when you take them from their sleeves
touch
hold

caress even

you poets

dreamers

lovers

in this place full of secrets

regrets

messy thoughts

just sometimes love

but always music

always music

aria sits in a little chair

over there, in the corner

under the faded enya-poster

and listens to vivaldi

donatella

she lives in the attic
high up above the bakery
donatella is an actor
wears a special mask
pretending to be someone else
today she's made tears and screams her focus
each wound must bleed again
or else the audience won't cry
every second sunday she heads to the cemetery
her tense brows knitted and
dark eyes in anguish finely fitted
the trick is not to be, but to become
a truly grieving parent for a baby son

resilience

there are days
when snow saddens everything away
hope
even goodness
a debilitating cold creep across the square
and aria's clothes grow damp to the skin
the fields outside town
still without any motion
aria hopes that bare trees
might teach her resilience —

yet when she thinks of her mother
on the whitening graveyard
a tear runs away past thinking
and for a moment
the cold slopes away
in silence

kieran

he did real estate for a while
but his accountant-heart beats stronger
urging Kieran to think in lines and rows
managing scarce resources
dreaming of benefits and costs
trying to satisfy his insatiable aspirations
always in a fight to beat the system
knowing that hurdles are prerequisites for success —
yet spreadsheets and tax returns
are no companions to beat loneliness
and so he heads to the bar
every night after work
hoping the pints might square the ledger
even if it is just for today

oblivious

the streets around the square
are filled with desire
with noise and shame
on some saturday nights
there they are
on the fringes
men, like drunken wolves, in half-light
women in fear
their lips moving in silent prayer
a policeman in the midst of it
oblivious to what is brewing
everyone knows everyone
but no one seems to care
about what is really going on

sleep

this evening
the sea greets you with gentle breath
as curtains fold against their will
children sleep
the smile of night on their faces
exchanging dreams with clouds
peaceful
stretched into dawn
so peaceful

in the morning
someone still sings a lullabye
hoping for a child
to still be just a child
for another day

humming

aria quietly hums an age-old tune
about the magic of the midnight hour
now it is the time to brave the world
with wisdom, certainty and power
she asks us if it's cowardly to leave your home
with no goodbyes
trying to forget what was

aria hums quietly
climbing up the willow
looking down at our world below
thatch roofs and some in shingles
streets, squares, fountains
fields and woods and cows by the river

now suddenly it is starting to snow

soon everything will freeze over

everything will stand still

everything will be suspended

in time

pure and white

aria hums quietly

climbing up the willow

About the Author

Joachim Matschoss, born in Germany, is living in Melbourne/Australia. He is a playwright, poet and Theatre-maker. His Theatre Company, 'Backyard Theatre Ensemble (BYTE)' presents diverse pieces of theatre nationally and internationally.

Joachim has created theatre in Australia, New Zealand, United Kingdom, India, Uzbekistan, Malaysia, Indonesia, Hong Kong, Hungary, Taiwan, Switzerland and China with various ensembles.

Joachim often works across art forms and in various languages.

Joachim's poetry is published in Australia, Germany, India, the United Kingdom and the USA.

He published a travel journal in Australia, *Away with me* and a novel in the USA, *Dead River Oaks*. A book about theatre and travel, *Rain Overnight*, has been published in India. His poetry is widely published. Collections include: *snow in december, a time heavy with life, geh ein stück mit, sidewalk theatre, stolpersteine*. A collection of his plays has been published in USA.

www.ingramcontent.com/pod-product-compliance
Lightning Source LLC
Chambersburg PA
CBHW020837150726
48196CB00002B/101